THE
UNCOMMON
MINISTER

**Power Principles
For Hitting Your
Target For Success
In Ministry**

VOLUME 1

MIKE MURDOCK

TABLE OF CONTENTS

The Uncommon Minister, Volume 1
Copyright © 1999 by Mike Murdock
ISBN 1-56394-100-7
Published by The Wisdom Center
P. O. Box 99 • Denton, Texas 76202

Unless otherwise indicated, all Scripture quotations are taken from the King James Version of the Bible.

To avoid the burdensome verbage of him/her; his, hers throughout this book, the simple reference to all of mankind, male or female, is simply "he" or "him."

WHY I WROTE THIS BOOK

I love preachers.

Everywhere I travel, I find ministers who are troubled, angry, sad and disappointed with their own progress in their ministry. Unreasonable goals, the trap of comparison with other ministries, mental exhaustion from trying to understand damaged congregations has often left us disillusioned about our own success for God. Yes, we are masters at disguising our disappointments, justifying unreached goals, and yet finding it impossible to get away from the ever present flame of hope within us...that God's potential could be unleashed at any time.

I was born into the ministry. My father pastored for 57 years. We had two family altars each day—morning and night. My mother insisted on the memorization of a Scripture every day of my life. I preached my first sermon at eight years of age in Waco, Texas, under my father's ministry. Later, at the age of nine, he permitted me to speak with him at various tent crusades. At the age of 15, friends of my father opened their doors for ministry to their congregations and youth groups. I attended Bible college for three semesters, then on February 9, 1966, I began my first evangelistic crusade as a young evangelist. That was over 30 years ago. After 38 countries and over 15,000 services, many Keys, Laws and Wisdom principles have become evident. Sitting at the supper table with the most uncommon ministers of my generation has unlocked many secrets—secrets that created "The Uncommon Minister."

Preachers are not alike.

Ministers are as different from each other as lawyers, fathers and salesmen.

Personalities differ. Goals are different. Their training is different. Their knowledge levels are different. Their pain is even different.

Doctors often cooperate for a mutual cause.

Lawyers often cooperate for a single benefit.

Farmers will link tractors to send a message to America.

Yet, ministers rarely cooperate together for a common cause. *It is among the greatest tragedies on earth that men who see the greatness of God rarely see the greatness in each other.*

Doctors are thrilled over the discoveries of another doctor. Actors will even hold annual celebration events to express recognition of the uniqueness of each.

Meanwhile, ministers of the gospel challenge, argue, stain and even publicly sneer at the discoveries, revelations or goals of another.

Still, the heavenly Father Who has *called* us, *anointed* us and *empowered* us to heal our broken generation insists we "love one another." Jesus said it clearly. "A new commandment I give unto you, That ye love one another; as I have loved you, that ye also love one another. By this shall all men know that ye are My disciples, if ye have love one to another" (John 13:34,35).

Anything God did not give you, He has carefully stored in someone near you. Love is the map to that Treasure.

Your ministry can become *satisfying* to you.

Your ministry can *multiply* in its effectiveness. Your ministry can become a *healing power*. Your ministry can become *greater* than ever. Your ministry can *increase in joy*. The Key? The Wisdom of God. *That's why I wrote this book.*

"Holy Spirit, use these simple words to unlock the greatness in the leaders you have chosen and anointed for my generation. Stir up the gift within us. Place Your coals of fire on our tongues, purify our words and strengthen our determination to walk in absolute obedience. Awaken a new passion for Your Word. Reveal steps that will unleash the waves of Wisdom for our people. Use us as Trophies of Divine Greatness to display what you can do with anyone who hears Your voice and obeys. In the name of Jesus, I pray. Amen."

"The Spirit of the Lord is upon me, because He hath anointed me to preach the gospel to the poor; He hath sent me to heal the brokenhearted, to preach deliverance to the captives, and recovering of sight to the blind, to set at liberty them that are bruised, to preach the acceptable year of the Lord" (Luke 4:18,19).

- Mike Murdock -

≈ 1 ≈

KNOW YOUR BIBLE.

————➤●◄————

The Word Of God is your life.
The Word of God is the greatest Book on earth.
It is the *revelation* of God. It is Truth. It is holy.
It is powerful. It heals. It energizes. It corrects.
It changes YOU.
The Word is the only Force that changes those who hear you.
When I was about 23 or 24 years old. I accepted an invitation for a crusade in Texas. The pastor had built one of the strongest churches ever in Houston, Texas.
Late one night, I ventured a question. "Would you critique and analyze my ministry for me? I respect you and truly want you to tell me what I am doing wrong or how I could I improve my ministry." (Actually, I was wanting him to affirm me and tell me all the things he liked about my ministry. But, he did not do that. He responded to the question I'd asked him.)
"Mike, in my early years, I had a ministry much like your own. Then, I went to England. The people patiently listened for a few months. Then, they began to approach me and tell me they appreciated my stories and illustrations, but they really had a desire to simply hear what the Word of God said about their problems and the solutions it offered."

He continued, "It hurt me deeply. But, when I went to prayer, God began to show me how to help the people become *dependent* upon the Word of God for their answers and solutions. Parables and stories were to confirm and reveal how the Word of God could be applied. But, they never got tired of hearing the Word of God and specific scriptures that applied to their lives."

He implied that my messages contained very few scriptures. He was correct. I cringed. It hurt. I was devastated emotionally. But, I was honest with myself and agreed that my messages were really two or three arguments and illustrations instead of the actual Word of God.

The Uncommon Minister must develop an obsession for understanding the mind of God. You see, the mind of God is revealed through the Word of God. His opinion of sin is revealed in the Word. His opinion of homosexuality is revealed in the Word. His opinion of prosperity is revealed in the Word. His guidelines for a productive life are revealed in the Word.

5 Helpful Keys Every Minister Should Remember

1. *Your Bible Is Your Wisdom Book, Not Your Sermon Book.* Many preachers only read the Scriptures while searching for a sermon for their people. It is not a part of their personal life.

2. *Read The Word Daily.* Habit will take you further than desire. Habitual exposure to the heart of God will create incredible results. When you read the biographies of uncommon spiritual leaders such

as Smith Wigglesworth and others—they had a *daily obsession* for the Word of God. It quickened and energized them. It lifted their spirits during times of oppression. It kept them *focused.* It *fueled* their hatred of sin and unleashed an *uncommon faith* in their own goals and Assignment.

3. *Personalize Your Bible By Marking Scriptures Impressing You.* I change Bibles each year. Every Bible has a different marking system. This year, I highlight in *yellow* every Scripture that I have memorized. *Red* marking is used for any truth concerning the Holy Spirit or the Word of God. *Green* marking concerns finances. *Blue* underlining occurs when a Scripture is worthy of reviewing, memorizing or using in a specific study.

4. *Tape Important Information On The Blank Pages In Your Bible.* Lowell Lundstrom, a long-time friend, opened his Bible one day to me. He had taped poems, biographical comments and powerful outlines from others throughout his Bible. His Bible was one of the most intriguing, fascinating and delightful books I had ever seen. It *excited* me. *Personalize* your Bible as your personal Success Handbook any way that you desire.

5. *Establish A Daily System For Reading Your Bible.* Several exist. Many years ago, I would read a small book (James or Titus) over and over again. Within a month, I would read the book of James 40 or 50 times. Imagine the incredible truths that began to leap off the pages! What you keep reading continually, you understand more completely.

Topical Study is selecting a particular topic and exhausting your research on it. Each morning for 30 days, I have taken a subject such as healing, the blood of Christ, or prosperity and marked every Scripture relating to it. It deepens your knowledge and enables you to even become an authority on that topic within a few months. Reading the Bible chronologically, Genesis through Revelation, is the most common way of reading the Scriptures. Three chapters a day and five on Sunday enable you to read the Bible through once a year. For many years, I have read 40 chapters a day. This enables me to complete the Bible every 30 days. It provides an overview that's remarkable. Whatever you do, *establish a system*. Change it when you desire. But, always have a system for reading the Word.

Know Your Bible.

It is One of the Secrets of The Uncommon Minister.

❧ 2 ❧

ENCOURAGE YOUR PEOPLE TO DISCOVER AND PURSUE THEIR OWN ASSIGNMENT.

———————⟐———————

Every person was created for a purpose.

Your people were created to become *Problem Solvers*. The problem they were created to solve is their *Assignment*. Dentists solve teeth problems. Lawyers solve legal problems. Mothers solve emotional problems.

As you minister, think about your people. Do you know the problems they were created to solve? Many pastors do not even know the jobs, careers or passions of their congregation. Sometimes, our messages do not quite relate to the specific goals and dreams of those we love and serve.

I flew to a crusade and was picked up by a very interesting young man, representing his pastor and church. As we drove to the hotel, he shared with me his dream. He longed to start his own business. The front seat was filled with books relating to his goals and dreams. He was very excited. He had been meeting with different mentors regarding this Assignment. I listened carefully. I asked numerous questions and that excited him. As he shared his goal, his face glowed. His conversation was animated and filled with genuine enthusiasm. He was building his whole life around his dream, that Assignment he felt so strong within him.

When I discussed this with his pastor the next day, the pastor seemed genuinely surprised.

"I've never really known quite what his business was about," the pastor confessed. "But, he has been attending our church for some time."

Several years ago, an elder in a church where I had ministered died. When she died, the pastor did not even know her address. He had never even shared a meal with her personally, though she had been on the staff for almost ten years.

He used her *gifts*.

He trusted her *judgment*.

He received her *offerings*.

But, he was uninterested in her own goals and dreams.

This is tragic. You see, *God did not create the people for the Ministry. God created the Ministry for the people.*

Your people need you.

Your people need your counsel concerning their Assignment, their goals and dreams. Move toward them. Secure their business cards and keep them in your Personal Prayer Book in your Secret Place.

5 Helpful Keys In Making Your Ministry More Effective In The Everyday Life And Routine Of Your People

1. *Remind Yourself Daily That Your Own Assignment As A Minister Is To Connect Your People To Their Assignment On The Earth.*

2. *Have Your People Complete A "Dreams And*

Goals Sheet." Keep it in notebooks in your Secret Place of prayer. Pray over those dreams and goals.

3. *Request A Business Card Or Photograph Of Their Personal Business Or Place Where They Work Each Day.* Keep that for times of intercession.

4. *Talk To Your People With A Genuine Desire To Understand Them In Light Of Their Own World.* You see, their world is *not* the Church. Their world is not preparing sermons for others. They face rejection, anger, temptation and hundreds of situations *without* a strong knowledge of the Word.

5. *Interrogate Them Continuously About Their Progress Towards Their Goals And Assignment.* Jesus did. Simon Peter went fishing. He caught nothing. When the morning was come, Jesus calls out, "Children, have ye any meat?" (Read John 21:5.) Jesus continuously showed an interest in *their* pain, *their* victories and *their* progress. Their pain was *His door* into their lives.

When you understand the needs, fears and goals of your people, your instructions to them can become more relevant, useable, pursued and celebrated. When the disciples expressed their loss to Jesus, He said simply, "Cast the net on the right side of the ship, and ye shall find" (John 21:6). You, too, can have this same impact.

Happy Sheep is the obsession of the Uncommon Shepherd. That is why the Great Shepherd instructed, "Feed my sheep." (See John 21:15-17.)

Encourage Your People To Discover And Pursue Their Own Assignment.

It is One of the Secrets of The Uncommon Minister.

≈ 3 ≈

DON'T OVERLOOK THE WOUNDED NEAREST YOU.

Focus often blinds you.

It is the "downside" of focus. It is the negative side of obsession for your calling. As a minister, you have goals and dreams. You become obsessed and focused. Your daily agenda revolves around that obsession. Every conversation contributes to that dream you are attempting to birth. You are fighting, clawing and exhausting every ounce of your being...to complete your Assignment on earth.

But, somebody near you is *hurting*.

They start withdrawing. They become introspective. Many times, they become reluctant to speak up. They see your stress, burdens and busyness. They feel unimportant, insignificant and unnecessary.

They believe any pursuit of your attention is considered an interruption or distraction. They *feel* it. They know it.

Your real ministry begins with those nearest you. That's why Jesus took His disciples aside, away from the multitude.

Those Who Minister For You Will Require Ministry From You.

Last night, this occurred to me. Three of us were working in my Wisdom Room on a project. I was consumed with a book. I had fought hard to preserve this private time, away from the pulpit and traveling. Suddenly, one of my staff began to cry. It dawned on me immediately that she had asked me several hours earlier to pray for her father. He was in a dangerous and critical condition in the hospital a thousand miles away. I had *intended* to pray for him, but my book was my obsession. As she sat there, her mind could not disconnect from the love she had for her father.

I was wrong. I had overlooked the needs of someone nearest me. I immediately stopped, apologized and called a special time of prayer.

Someone who never causes trouble is usually ignored. This occurred to me some months ago. My general manager mentioned a very difficult situation one of the staff members was facing. I was stunned. They had been living with this problem for a long time. I had not known it. Why? She was not a complainer, not a whiner. She was a thankful person. She was *not* a reacher. She was *not* a manipulator, maneuvering everyone toward the solution of her problem. She was quiet, shy and *alone*. Others who had experienced similar problems were often demanding, vocal and outspoken. So they received the attention they wanted. Quiet children need attention as much as opinionated children. Yet, they are often overlooked.

Your most supportive people will seldom reveal their deepest needs and wounds. While praying recently, the Holy Spirit reminded me of one of the staff members. "When did they receive their last raise?" I asked my general manager.

"I don't really know," was her reply. "But, I will find out."

She had not received a raise in over two years of working for the ministry. She had never complained. She had never griped. But I had overlooked her needs.

My mail often piles up. Phone calls pour in by the hundreds to my office every week. Everyone seems to be in crisis.

Too often we respond to the loudest.

Too often we respond to the most obnoxious.

Too often we respond to the most persistent.

That's why the families of ministers are often the last to receive our attention. Our staff is often the last to receive our favor.

Those nearest us should be the first to receive the fruit of our love, blessings and attention.

Who needs a special season of *restoration* and relaxation? Who needs a *listening* ear? Who is being ignored by others? Who is in a true financial crisis? "Withhold not good from them to whom it is due, when it is in the power of thine hand to do it" (Proverbs 3:27).

Don't Overlook The Wounded Nearest You.

It is One of the Secrets of The Uncommon Minister.

≈ 4 ≈

CONTINUALLY REVIEW AND UPDATE YOUR MINISTRY GOALS.

Your ministry goals will change continuously.
Someday, you will look back at this very moment and be amazed at the goals you presently have. Things so vital to you at 20 years old will become unimportant to you at 30.

When I was beginning my ministry, I wanted very much to minister in many different states and cities. For some reason, it made me feel successful, desired and accepted when I received invitations from many *different* places. Today, staying home excites me! Knowing that my books are being read in many places is more satisfying to me than traveling.

The greatest goal of my life today is staying in my Secret Place of prayer and writing what the Holy Spirit teaches me.

I remember well the excitement over hiring my first secretary. At last, someone would help me do all the typing! Today, 31 associates here at my offices work diligently around the clock producing and processing mail, books, tapes and videos. Times have changed. Needs have changed. My personal goals have changed.

It will happen to you, too.

Your present feelings are not permanent. Your present opinions are probably temporary. Your present views have been sculptured by your past experiences. New experiences are coming. New relationships are ahead. Stay conscious of this. *Never make permanent decisions because of temporary feelings.*

15 Keys Concerning Your Dreams And Goals

1. *Recognize That Others Cannot Discern What Is Important To You At This Point.* You alone can decide what generates your joy. Have you ever been agitated when someone became too aggressive or pushy in trying to get you to bowl, play tennis or golf when you knew those things did not excite you? You see, people want you to enjoy what *they* like!

Few friends will ever understand your unique tastes, desires and excitements. Some love parties while others prefer a prayer meeting. Some love shopping, others love studying.

2. *Discern And Treasure Anything Or Anyone That Energizes And Motivates You.* Reading, motorcycles, travel, learning another language, working in your flower garden, painting, shopping, or playing golf. Name it to yourself. Know what you love. *Know what you truly enjoy.* You see, few people really do know the things that they enjoy. They *watch* life instead of *living* life. Millions stare at a television set day after day without having any idea of the life they could live personally. They are watching *others* live the life they covet.

3. *Stop Apologizing To Those Who Don't*

Understand What You Love. I have an insatiable desire to learn. Reading excites me. Something drives me to write books. When I complete a book, I feel exhilarated. Thrilled. Excited. I feel progress when I dictate a significant portion of a book.

Many friends do not grasp this sensitivity within me. They urge me to "play golf." I do not understand golfers. While many of my friends enjoy hitting a small ball hundreds of yards, then hitting it further and further for hours—it baffles me. I don't understand the fascination of golfing.

They don't understand my fascination with learning! So, when they drop by my office, they always want to preach me a little sermon on the importance of "relaxing." *Their discussion on relaxing is more stressful than anything else I am doing!* While I'm listening to their boring and uninteresting lecture on "taking time off," I could be generating incredible joy and progress through dictation on a book. They are attempting to be helpful. Actually, I consider them a distraction!

4. *Do Not Depend On Others To Understand Your Dreams And Goals.* Permit them *their* individuality. They have every right to love the things they love. But refuse to be intimidated by their efforts to persuade you to adopt their lifestyle.

5. *Accept That Many May Not Celebrate What You Are Pursuing.* They do not treasure those things that are important to you. This can be heartbreaking when those you love seem disinterested.

6. *Determine What Matters To You More Than Anything Else.* Your spiritual goals must become the *most* important goals. Your financial dreams require attention. Your physical goals deserve

attention as well.

7. *Invest One Hour In Writing Down Clearly The Things That Really Matter To You At This Point.* You can keep it confidential, private and away from prying eyes. You must *continuously* assess and evaluate any *changing* of goals you are experiencing in your ministry.

8. *Permit Unexciting Dreams Of Yesterday To Die.* Stop pursuing something that does not have the ability to excite you anymore. Don't feel obligated to keep attempting to obtain it...if you are now in a different place in your life. Perhaps, you wanted to own a motorcycle ten years ago. You never bought one. Now, you have the money to purchase it, but the excitement over it has died. Don't buy it now! That season has passed. Permit it to die.

9. *Don't Expect Everyone On Your Staff To Always Pursue Great Dreams For Themselves.* You cannot *force* them. *Encourage* them. But you cannot *force* greatness on anyone.

Several years ago, I became excited about helping some of my staff achieve maximum physical fitness. Purchasing a special building, I filled it with the best workout equipment available. Then, I hired a special trainer ($75 an hour) to give personal attention and teaching. Within three weeks, only two showed up. Each had their own excuse for not working out. It was across the street from the office. It did not cost anyone a cent. Yet, I could not force it on them.

I have a beautiful gym at my home. It contains a wonderful basketball court, workout areas, and is ideal for a top physical fitness program. Yet, the friends closest to me continually give excuses when I ask them to come work out with me. The only person encouraging me is my trainer! Occasionally, I hold a self-pity party for myself. Sometimes, I feel somewhat alone in my huge gym. But, it keeps me reminded that you cannot force others to grow their own Seeds of Greatness.

Success is an individual decision. Nobody else can make it for you. You cannot make it for anyone else either.

You may become discouraged from being the only person in your family making a maximum effort. Working out alone is not fun. But, let me encourage you to grow the picture of your dream bigger...bigger and bigger. Don't quit. Determine to experience your dream whether anyone else around you experiences it or not.

10. *Understand That Others May Need To See You Succeed First.* Many become demoralized and discouraged with themselves. They want to see you succeed *before* they make any attempts again. As you give yourself to your goals, something can catch fire within them.

11. *Avoid Intimate Relationships With Those Who Do Not Really Respect Your Dreams.* You will have to sever ties. *Wrong people do not always leave your life voluntarily.* I have experienced friends sitting in my gym, laughing at me trying to develop myself. They have attempted to "talk me out of body building." You don't need anyone close to you raining on your parade. Life is too short to permit discouragers close to you.

12. *Place Photographs Of Your Desired Future On The Walls Around You.* "Write the vision, make it plain on tables that he may run that readeth it" (Habakkuk 2:2). Write your dreams. Put pictures around you. They motivate you.

13. *You Must Learn The Secret Of Encouraging Yourself In Your Ministry.* Avoid the presence of cynics, critics and faultfinders. Your own family may find reasons you should quit, lower your goals and try something easier. Don't fall for it. Stay focused.

14. *Choose Your Friends Instead Of Letting Your Friends Choose You.*

15. *Identify Those Who Have Become Burdens Instead Of Burden Bearers.* Some enter your life with a "desire to help." Within weeks, they have become burdens instead. Analyze and evaluate on a consistent basis those who have become difficult, obnoxious and troublesome. Then identify those who really lift the burdens from your life. Celebrate them. Provide access. Avoid permitting them to overwork themselves. Good people can become burdensome to us if we do not protect them as well.

When you assess and evaluate your goals, you will unclutter your life of the unnecessary.

Continually Review And Update Your Ministry Goals.

It is One of the Secrets of The Uncommon Minister.

∾ 5 ∾

Treasure Your Ministry Mailing List.

Friendship is a golden gift from God.

When I was 18 years old, I spoke in a small country church in Louisiana. At the close of the service, the pastor approached me.

"I noticed you are selling your records. My son takes the name and address of every person who purchases his album. So, when he produces a new album, his previous customers always purchase his new one immediately. Son, you ought to start collecting the names of every person who hears you minister."

Well, I was 18. An *ignorant* 18. I didn't want to take the time to do it. So, I did not do it...until I was almost 30 years old. That's when I started seriously considering documenting the names of every person who had sat under my ministry. That pastor's son? He ended up selling millions and millions of records and tapes throughout the world. He became one of the most famous names throughout Christianity.

He knew the importance of a name.

Three men flew from Phoenix, Arizona, to my home in Houston, Texas, when I was about 30 years old. They had analyzed my ministry. They declared that I was "destined for significance" and wanted to participate in my growing ministry. They had quite a resume. Two of the most powerful ministries in the United States had hired them in previous years. They questioned me about my "mailing list." Well, I really did not have a serious mailing list. When someone wrote me, I answered. But, I did not keep constant and regular contact with them.

"How many monthly partners do you have in your ministry?" they asked.

I confessed that I did not have *any* monthly partners. Explaining that I was a *church* evangelist, I told them that most pastors did not want the names of their people given to evangelists. In fact, one major pastor had complimented me saying, "I really appreciate that you never ask for financial help for your ministry. If you did, I would not allow you to put out your newsletter on the table in my church. I do not want my people writing other ministries."

As I explained this to them, they asked another penetrating question.

"Do you have *enough finances* to do *everything* God has told you to do with your ministry?"

"Of course not," I replied. "I don't even have enough money to hire a secretary or rent an office. My present office is in my garage."

"Then, how will you ever be able to complete your instructions from God *without partners* to help you financially?"

It angered me. They were correct, of course. But, I had taken *great pride in the fact that I never asked for financial help*. Pastors had even expressed their appreciation of this. No, I did not have one single monthly partner. I simply traveled night after night, week after week, year after year pouring my life out.

Whatever was given me as an offering, I lived on. Yet, I did not have enough money to publish books, make cassette tapes or even purchase a home. The offerings were simply enough to buy gasoline, a car and keep traveling day after day.

These consultants told me bluntly and boldly that my ministry would never succeed significantly *until I valued the names of those who cared*, potential partners who could help me spread this gospel. I became belligerent, and invited them to leave my home.

Some months later, I sat at my desk with work overwhelming me. I desperately needed a secretary. My garage was crammed full of boxes. That's when I realized I had to overcome my pride, *write* my closest friends and ask for their *monthly* support.

That was the beginning of explosive growth.

A number of my friends wrote back and agreed to assist me. A secretary was hired. My first office was established. The songs, the books and the teaching tapes began to roll through me...because I truly valued those God had brought into my life and ministry.

Every successful pastor knows the importance of a name. That's why visitor cards are given out each service. Receptions where greeters meet newcomers are held every Sunday morning. Millions of dollars are spent on television programs, radio broadcasts and newspaper ads, because *people* are important to your vision.

Every successful businessman knows the importance of a single name. Listen to Ron Popeil, a multimillionaire who has succeeded greatly. "One of the mandates at Ronco, beside quality and innovation, is this: A name, address, and phone number are worth gold. We always capture a telephone number in addition to the name and address of a customer, because those items are very common, very valuable." (Page 219, "The Salesman of the Century.")

Friendships are too precious to lose. They cost too much to treat lightly. I read once where former President George Bush had 7,500 names on his Rolodex files. He loves people. He values people. He knows the importance of a name.

Treasure Your Ministry Mailing List.

It is One of the Secrets of The Uncommon Minister.

≈ 6 ≈

SCHEDULE DIVINE DEPOSITS THROUGH THE TAPES OF UNCOMMON ACHIEVERS.

You must receive before you give.

Last night, I flew in from a crusade in Houston. I arrived at 9:30 p.m., but had to remain on the runway for a long time due to early arrival. It was midnight when I finally arrived home. Though tired, I ran my bath water and relaxed. The day had been a full one. I did not feel like reading, cleaning up my house or anything else. But I knew the power of simply *listening.* So, I played a cassette tape of one of the most effective business writers in America. He was conducting an interview with a major motivation speaker. It was tremendous. Though I was too fatigued to study, my time for bathing and getting ready for bed was not wasted. The tape was still playing when I drifted off to sleep an hour later.

Mentorship can take place any moment of the day when you plan ahead for such opportunities.

While getting dressed, you can listen to tapes.

While cleaning your room, you can listen to a mentorship tape.

If you eat lunch alone, this is an ideal time to

receive special teaching from someone, listening to a cassette.

Mentorship is so important. Mentors are those who know something you do not know. They have been where you want to go. They have accomplished something significant that you admire. Most Uncommon Achievers care deeply about others and long to impart their secrets to them.

Don't lose these moments.

7 Keys Every Minister Should Know About Personal Mentorship

1. *Listen To Your Mentorship Tapes More Than Once.* I discovered early that I rarely heard everything on a tape when I listened the first time. Listening several times revealed that I had missed important information on the first or second listening.

2. *When You Hear Something Vital And Essential, Stop The Tape And Play It Back Again Immediately.* When you keep listening to it, it will get inside your spirit and heart.

3. *Write, In A Special Notebook, Those Things You Want To Remember From The Tape.*

4. *Stop And Picture The Truth That Is Taking Place.* Visualization is a powerful way to *keep something that you're hearing.* (Read Habakkuk 2:2.)

5. *Talk To Other Ministers About The Secret You Learned.* Discuss it, and how it can apply to their ministry.

6. *Keep The Mentorship Tapes Visible And Accessible.* Take advantage of every spare moment.

7. *Listen To A Variety Of Mentors.* Do not limit yourself to one school of thought. Listen to

businessmen. Listen to motivational speakers. Listen to cassette tapes of missionaries, pastors and evangelists. Every person has been given a different view and has experienced a variation of events in their lives.

Learn from many. The Holy Spirit used 40 different authors over a 1,600-year period to document the Scriptures. Each author was inspired to focus on something different...*for a reason.*

Schedule Divine Deposits Through The Tapes Of Uncommon Achievers.

It is One of the Secrets of The Uncommon Minister.

≈ 7 ≈

GIVE ATTENTION TO THE OFFERINGS OF YOUR PEOPLE.

━━━━━━━⇒⊋●⊆⇐━━━━

Offerings matter to God.
Offerings matter to *people*.
Offerings *should* matter to *you*.
It is the Uncommon Minister of the gospel, who willingly unlocks provision for the body of Christ.

6 Keys Every Minister Should Remember About Offerings

1. *Recognize The Importance Of An Offering To God.* Think of many Scriptures where God carefully explains the value and future of the sowing of His people. He even listed various kinds of offerings such as the trespass offering, the peace offering, the sin offering, and even the tithe! (Read Malachi 3:8-12.)

2. *Recognize That The Offerings Of Your People Are Deciding Their Future.* Their Seeds determine their harvest. Your ministry and celebration of their Seed will affect their opinion of their giving. "*Honour* the Lord with thy substance, and with the firstfruits of all thine increase: So shall thy barns be filled with plenty, and thy presses shall burst out with new wine" (Proverbs 3:9,10).

3. *Teach Your People To Treasure The Moment Of Sowing.* Jesus stood and watched the widow give all she had. God assigned a prophet to one widow just to help her unlock the Seed for her harvest. (See 1 Kings 17.)

4. *Remember That Any Attention You Give To The Seeds Of The People Affects Their View Of Its Importance.* When you make statements like, "I wish we never had to receive offerings," you have just belittled and possibly destroyed the impact of their Seed.

5. *Make The Moment Of Bringing An Offering To God An Unforgettable Portrait Of Blessing In The Hearts Of Your Families.* One of my dear friends in Pennsylvania has an event at every service during the offering. He places several offering containers on the steps of the platform. Each family comes as a unit, standing at the offering container and praying together over their Seed. When they have finished praying over their Seed, they place it in the offering container and return to their seats. Then, the next family moves up behind them. There are several rows of people giving. It is a most holy, sacred and unforgettable moment of receiving offerings.

6. *Never Rush The Offering Of The People To Their God.* You don't rush the choir. You don't rush the announcement about the baseball games. Why would you rush the Thanksgiving Moment that occurs only three times in a seven-day period?

Give Attention To The Offerings Of Your People.

It is One of the Secrets of the Uncommon Minister.

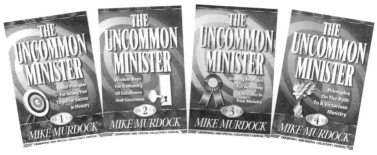

Complete your personal library of
"The Uncommon Minister" Series. These first seven
volumes are a must for your ministry reading.
Practical and powerful, these Wisdom Keys will
enhance your ministry expression for years to come.

ITEM	TITLE	QTY	PRICE	TOTAL
B107	The Uncommon Minister, Volume 1		$5.00	$
B108	The Uncommon Minister, Volume 2		$5.00	$
B109	The Uncommon Minister, Volume 3		$5.00	$
B110	The Uncommon Minister, Volume 4		$5.00	$
B111	The Uncommon Minister, Volume 5		$5.00	$
B112	The Uncommon Minister, Volume 6		$5.00	$
B113	The Uncommon Minister, Volume 7		$5.00	$
All 7 Volumes of The Uncommon Minister			$35.00	$

Mail To:
The Wisdom Center
P.O. Box 99
Denton, TX 76202
940-891-1400

Add 10% For Shipping	$
(Canada add 20% to retail cost and 20% shipping)	$
Enclosed Is My Seed-Faith Gift For Your Ministry	$
Total Amount Enclosed	$

SORRY NO C.O.D.'S

Name _____
Address _____
City _____
State _____
Zip _____ Telephone _____

☐ Check ☐ Money Order
☐ Visa ☐ Master Card ☐ Amex
Signature _____
Exp. Date _____
Card No. _____

THE
WISDOM
CENTER

―――――――― **Quantity Prices for** ――――――――
"The Uncommon Minister" Series

1-9	=	$5.00 each
10-99	=	$4.00 each (20% discount)
100-499	=	$3.50 each (30% discount)
500-999	=	$3.00 each (40% discount)
1,000-up	=	$2.50 each (50% discount)
5,000-up	=	$2.00 each (60% discount)

WISDOM 12 PAK

THE MASTER SECRET OF LIFE IS WISDOM

Ignorance Is The Only True Enemy Capable Of Destroying You (Hosea 4:6, Proverbs 11:14)

▸	1.	MY PERSONAL DREAM BOOK	B143	$5.00
▸	2.	THE COVENANT OF FIFTY EIGHT BLESSINGS	B47	$8.00
▸	3.	WISDOM, GOD'S GOLDEN KEY TO SUCCESS	B71	$7.00
▸	4.	SEEDS OF WISDOM ON THE HOLY SPIRIT	B116	$5.00
▸	5.	SEEDS OF WISDOM ON THE SECRET PLACE	B115	$5.00
▸	6.	SEEDS OF WISDOM ON THE WORD OF GOD	B117	$5.00
▸	7.	SEEDS OF WISDOM ON THE ASSIGNMENT	B122	$5.00
▸	8.	SEEDS OF WISDOM ON PROBLEM SOLVING	B118	$5.00
▸	9.	101 WISDOM KEYS	B45	$7.00
▸	10.	31 KEYS TO A NEW BEGINNING	B48	$7.00
▸	11.	THE PROVERBS 31 WOMAN	B49	$7.00
▸	12.	31 FACTS ABOUT WISDOM	B46	$7.00

Wisdom Is The Principal Thing

Book Pak
WBL-12 / **$30**

(A $73 Value!)

The Wisdom Center

ORDER TODAY!
www.thewisdomcenter.cc

1-888-WISDOM-1
(1-888-947-3661)

THE WISDOM CENTER • P.O. Box 99 • Denton, Texas 76202

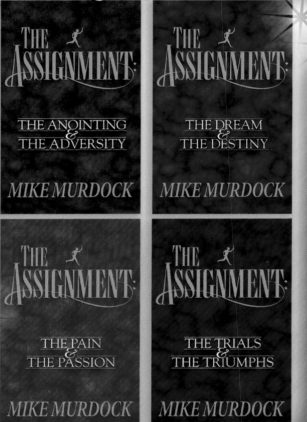

The Secret Place
Library Pak

Songs from the Secret Place

Over 40 Great Songs On 6 Music Tapes
Including "I'm In Love" / Love Songs From The Holy Spirit
Birthed In The Secret Place / Side A Is Dr. Mike Murdock
Singing / Side B Is Music Only For Your Personal Prayer Time

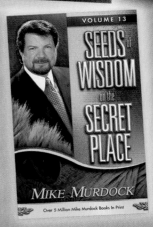

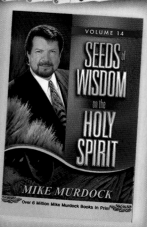

Seeds of Wisdom on the Secret Place

4 Secrets The Holy Spirit Reveals In The Secret Place / The Necessary
Ingredients In Creating Your Secret Place / 10 Miracles That Will
Happen In The Secret Place

Seeds of Wisdom on the Holy Spirit

The Protocol For Entering The Presence Of
The Holy Spirit / the greatest day of my life and
What Made It So / Power Keys For Developing Your
Personal Relationship With The Holy Spirit

Wisdom Is The Principal Thing
Book/Tape Pak
SP PAK-001 / $30
Six Audio Tapes & Two Books
(A $40 Value!)
The Wisdom Center

ORDER TODAY!
www.thewisdomcenter.cc

1-888-WISDOM-1
(1-888-947-3661)

THE WISDOM CENTER • P.O. Box 99 • Denton, Texas 76202

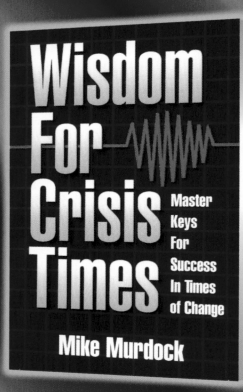

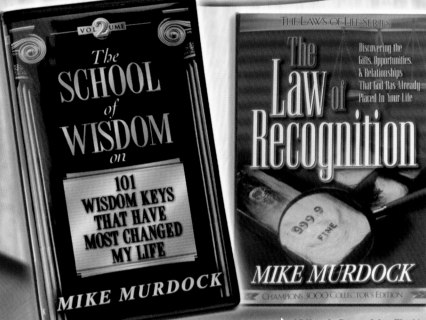

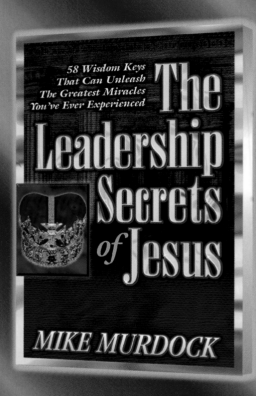

Your Rewards In Life Are Determined By The Problems You Solve.

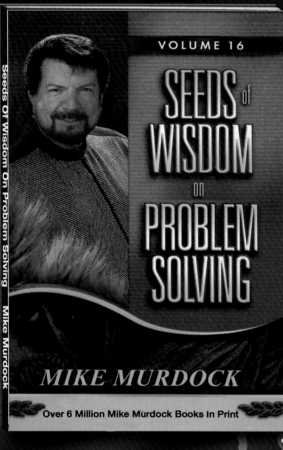

VOLUME 16

SEEDS of WISDOM on PROBLEM SOLVING

Seeds Of Wisdom On Problem Solving — Mike Murdock

MIKE MURDOCK

Over 6 Million Mike Murdock Books In Print

▸ *3 Simple Ways To Increase Your Income In 90 Days*

▸ *4 Keys To Recognizing The Problems You Were Created To Solve*

▸ *12 Rewards Received When You Solve Problems For Others*

▸ *5 Important Keys To Remember When You Face A Problem*

▸ *2 Ways You Will Be Remembered*

▸ *12 Keys to Becoming An Uncommon Problem Solver*

▸ *6 Keys To Establishing Your Legacy*

Wisdom Is The Principal Thing

Book B-118 / **$5**

The Wisdom Center

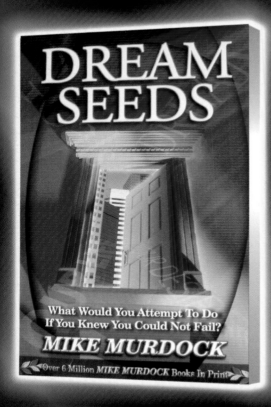

Where You Are Determines What Grows In You.

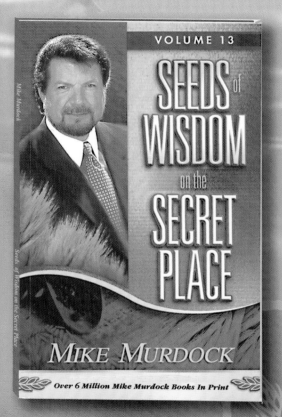

VOLUME 13

SEEDS of WISDOM on the SECRET PLACE

MIKE MURDOCK

Over 6 Million Mike Murdock Books In Print

▸ 4 Secrets The Holy Spirit Reveals In The Secret Place

▸ Master Keys in Cultivating An Effective Prayer Life

▸ The Necessary Ingredients In Creating Your Secret Place

▸ 10 Miracles That Will Happen In The Secret Place

Wisdom Is The Principal Thing

Book B-115 / $5

The Wisdom Center

Run To Win.

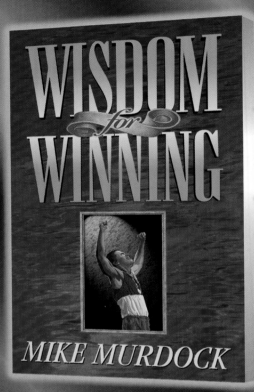

- 10 Ingredients For Success
- Ten Lies Many People Believe About Money
- 20 Keys For Winning At Work
- 20 Keys To A Better Marriage
- 3 Facts Every Parent Should Remember
- 5 Steps Out Of Depression
- The Greatest Wisdom Principle I Ever Learned
- 7 Keys To Answered Prayer
- God's Master Golden Key To Total Success
- The Key To Understanding Life

Everyone needs to feel they have achieved something with their life. When we stop producing, loneliness and laziness will choke all enthusiasm from our living. What would you like to be doing? What are you doing about it? Get started on a project in your life. Start building on your dreams. Resist those who would control and change your personal goals. Get going with this powerful teaching and reach your life goals!

THE WISDOM CENTER

ORDER TODAY!
www.thewisdomcenter.cc

1-888-WISDOM-1
(1-888-947-3661)

THE WISDOM CENTER • P.O. Box 99 • Denton, Texas 76202

THE SECRET.

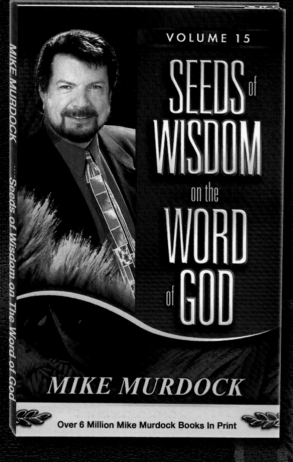

VOLUME 15

SEEDS of WISDOM on the WORD of GOD

MIKE MURDOCK

Over 6 Million Mike Murdock Books In Print

MIKE MURDOCK · Seeds of Wisdom on The Word of God

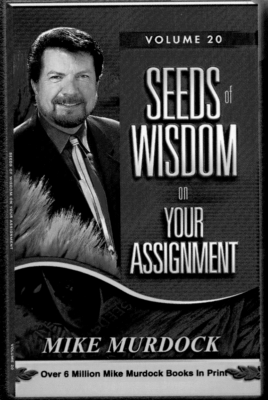

WISDOM COLLECTION

8

SECRETS OF THE UNCOMMON MILLIONAIRE

1. The Uncommon Millionaire Conference Vol. 1 (Six Cassettes)
2. The Uncommon Millionaire Conference Vol. 2 (Six Cassettes)
3. The Uncommon Millionaire Conference Vol. 3 (Six Cassettes)
4. The Uncommon Millionaire Conference Vol. 4 (Six Cassettes)
5. 31 Reasons People Do Not Receive Their Financial Harvest (256 Page Book)
6. Secrets of the Richest Man Who Ever Lived (178 Page Book)
7. 12 Seeds of Wisdom Books On 12 Topics
8. The Gift of Wisdom for Leaders Desk Calendar
9. Songs From The Secret Place (Music Cassette)
10. In Honor of the Holy Spirit (Music Cassette)
11. 365 Memorization Scriptures On The Word Of God (Audio Cassette)

Wisdom Is The Principal Thing
THE WISDOM COLLECTION 8
SECRETS OF THE UNCOMMON MILLIONAIRE
WC-08 / $195
The Wisdom Center